GEORGE PRATT
NO MAN'S LAND

A POSTWAR SKETCHBOOK

OF THE WAR IN THE TRENCHES

Introduction by Marshall Arisman

Tundra Publishing Ltd.

1992

edited by Greg S. Baisden
book design by George Pratt & Tamara Sibert

FOREWORD

In 1988 or so, I was hard at work on an anti-war graphic novel titled *Enemy Ace: War Idyll*. The majority of the book centered on one man, Hans von Hammer, and his remembrances and perceptions of the First World War. The project was the largest I had ever attempted and occupied vast amounts of my time. As I read more and more about the conflict and the men who fought it, I found myself totally consumed by the visual and emotional impulses the stories prompted in me.

The sketches in this book, then, were almost all created to train my eye to see into that dim black-and-white world that was the First World War. They began as a way of learning the costumes of that era, the way cloth folds over an arm in that manner particular to heavy wool. What the sketches ultimately became was a private refuge, a place to put all the painting behind me and dwell only in line and that specific simplicity that can only be achieved with line. The spontaneity, the fluidity of drawing straight with a pen, trying to capture life with as few strokes as possible.

What aided me immensely in this especially was my subway sketching. I sketch constantly. I'm never without a sketchbook. It's like breathing, yet it is not the deep exhalations of a long distance runner, but rather the fast, controlled hyperventilation of the sprinter. You have to move fast. The person you are sketching will, most likely, get up in less than a minute, so you fly, race against time to capture the essence of that frozen moment, not quite so frozen.

Of course, most of this is analysis, which for me is the antithesis of drawing, sketching. The bottom line (no pun intended) is that art is life, line is life. That is why I also love to watch others draw. It is magic. It seems so effortless for them, as if they are literally tracing an image projected on the page before them. For me, it is a daily struggle, but one I happily embrace and enjoy.

The monotypes also fall into this love I have for spontaneity and mood. A monotype is to the oil painter what the quick sketch or doodle is to the penman, a *gavotte* with the medium itself.

A monotype is produced by creating a thin oil painting on the surface of an etching plate or piece of plexiglass. This plate is then placed face-up on an etching press with a sheet of dry or moistened paper laid on top. The two are covered with blankets and cranked through the press. The result is a single reversed impression of the painting, which can be taken as is or reworked with oil, acrylic, watercolor, or even pen and ink. There is a certain look and feel specific to a monotype. They assimilate all the visual entrapments of oil painting, etching, and drawing, and beautifully, powerfully unite them. For that very reason, I consider my monotypes to be some of my most successful pieces, and the medium itself one of the most enjoyable. You never really know what you're going to get with a monotype. Peeling the print from the plate is a moment of great anticipation (for it is almost like seeing the work of someone else) and pleasure.

I came to monotypes at the end of *Enemy Ace* and saw it as the perfect way to enhance the chapter headings of that book. Happily, I discovered that the medium had applications far beyond that one project—specifically, my own personal expression regardless of any commercial aspects. I absolutely love the act of printmaking and surrender myself more and more to its splendid subtleties.

The work within this book captures a very specific time in my life where I grew both emotionally and artistically. It was a period of great upheavals for me, but the work and the wonderful artists that I am lucky enough to call friends pulled me through it all. This book is dedicated to all of them. Enjoy.

George Pratt
Brooklyn, NY
July 1992

INTRODUCTION

Artists have used drawings to record events, particularly wars, since the beginning of recorded history. In the mid-seventeenth century, the Japanese developed the hand-scroll to illustrate military exploits and court life. The discovery of lithography opened new doors for mass publication of recorded images and developed a vigorous popular press. By the nineteenth century, the artist/reporter had become a major factor in satisfying the enormous hunger for information. *Harper's Weekly* and *Frank Leslie's Illustrated Newspaper* employed 26 artists to report the American Civil War.

The role of documenting wars through drawing changed with the perfection of the new Kodak pocket camera in 1895. The camera proved to be faster, cheaper, and a more reliable tool for documentation. Consequently, artists were pushed to explore more personal visions of war and its effect upon the people who fought them.

World War I, with all of its horrors, became subject matter for a group of German artists whose impact on the art world continued into the 1920s and 1930s. The work of Otto Dix, Max Beckmann, and George Grosz still stands as a monument against war. Max Beckmann stated, "The more frequently one died, the more intensely one lived. I drew—that is what kept me from dying."

What I find quite remarkable about the drawings in this book is that they were done in the past two years by a young American artist. George Pratt was not an eyewitness. George Pratt was not in World War I. In fact, to my knowledge, George Pratt was never in a war. The windows of his studio in Brooklyn look out upon the homeless, not upon the trenches of Europe. That is part of what makes this series of drawings so fascinating.

His ability to convince the viewer that these drawings were done "on the spot" is a tribute to his artistic capabilities. He is committed to a new form in the United States called the graphic novel, series of pictures and words that recreate periods of time with total believability. The letters and poetry he has chosen for this book form the basis of his visual essay.

Howard Pyle, often called the Father of American Illustration, stated repeatedly that the primary task for the illustrator is to believe the pictures are, in fact, true. If the artist creating the pictures doesn't believe them, then why should the viewer?

George Pratt has taken this advice to heart. Placing himself in *No Man's Land*, he has taken us there as well. We share this experience together. George Pratt has managed to achieve a synthesis of what he observes and what he imagines to be true.

This book establishes his drawings as part of an exciting approach to the concept of what it means to be an eyewitness. It does, in fact, redefine the term.

Marshall Arisman

THE SKETCHES

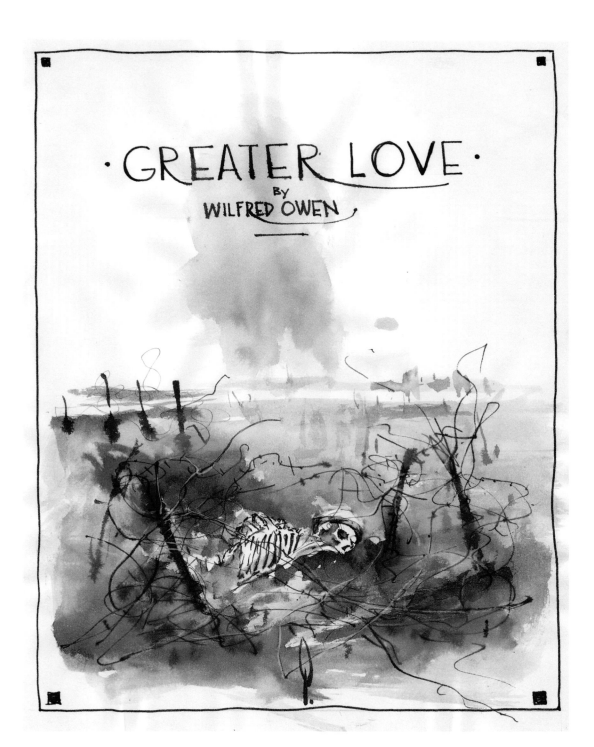

Red Lips are not so red
  As the stained stones kissed by the English dead.

Kindness of wooed and wooer
Seems shame to their love pure.
O Love, your eyes lose lure
  When I behold eyes blinded in my stead!

Your slender attitude
    Trembles not exquisite like limbs knife-skewed,
Rolling and rolling there
Where God seems not to care;
Till the fierce love they bear
    Cramps them in death's extreme decreptitude.

Your voice sings not so soft, —
  Though even as wind murmuring through raftered loft, —
Your dear voice is not dear,
Gentle, and evening clear,
  As theirs whom none now hear,
  Now earth has stopped their piteous mouths that coughed.

Heart, you were never hot
    Nor large, nor full like hearts made great with shot;
And though your hand be pale,
Paler are all which trail
Your cross through flame and hail:
    Weep, you may weep, for you may touch them not.

The War that will end War.

H.G.Wells

There has been great difficulty in making many eligible men understand that their services are urgently required, and there have never been wanting pestilential persons who insidiously hinder recruiting.

The Times

Despite all my hatred and aversion for war, I should not have liked to have missed the memory of those first days. As never before, thousands and thousands felt what they should have felt in peacetime—that they belonged together.

Stefan Zweig, 1914

Nearly every red-blooded human boy has had war, in some shape or form, for his first love; if his blood has remained red and he has kept some of his boyishness in afterlife, that first love will never have been forgotten.

Saki, 1915

Oxford colleges have just begun their Christmas term. There will be about 250 freshmen as compared with 571 last year. The average number of freshmen between 1910 and 1913 was 934. Keble College has the largest number of freshmen with 22.

Daily Mail (Overseas Edition), 23 October 1915

The whole idea was to get hold of a rifle, learn to shoot a bit, proceed to France at the earliest possible moment, kill vast quantities of Germans, possibly get wounded in some artistic place, win the war, and march back with Colours flying and bands playing and the girls falling on your neck.

Captain Alan Goring, MC

Modern history affords no such example of a great nation running amok and calling it military necessity.

New York World

Germany is the only possiblity for the further spiritual development of man.

General Count von Moltke the younger

When zero hour arrived, the officer would blow a whistle. If you didn't hear it, you saw everybody mounting the parapet so you did the same and on you went, with the best of luck and a spoonful of rum.

Corporal J.G.Mortimer, MM

The old earth of the battlefields is thirsty for the wine of our blood.
Padraic Pearse, 1916

When a butcher tells you that his heart "bleeds for his country" be has in fact no uneasy feeling.

Dr. Johnson, Voices From The Great War

Kill a good few for me.

Ethel Munro, to her brother Saki

A battle is an amazing mixture of Hell and a family picnic—not as frightening as the dentist, but absorbing, sometimes thrilling like football, sometimes dull like church, and sometimes simply physically sickening, like bad fish. Burying dead afterwards is worst of all.

Hugh Walpole, to Arnold Bennett

In the newspapers you read:
"Peacefully they rest on the spot where they have bled and suffered, while the guns roar over their graves, taking vengeance for their heroic death." And it doesn't occur to anybody that the enemy is also firing; that the shells plunge into the hero's grave; that his bones are mingled with the filth which they scatter to the four winds—and that, after a few weeks, the morass closes over the last resting-place of the soldier.

Kanonier Gerhardt Gürtler, 111 Bavarian Corps Artillerie

Pressed close against each other
The dead without hatred or flag
The hair stiff with congealed blood
The dead are all on one side
René Arcos, The Dead

Put out that bloody cigarette.

Saki (H.H. Munro), last words before
being killed by a German sniper, 1916

If any question why we died
Tell them—because our fathers lied.

Rudyard Kipling, 1915, on learning that his
son John had been killed on the western front

But it is a commentary on modern war that commanders should fear lest the soldiers on each side become friendly. Our soldiers have no quarrel with "Fritz," save during the heat of battle, or in retaliation for some blow below the belt. If whole armies fraternised, politicians on both sides would be sore set to solve their problems. Yet it is possible that if there had been a truce for a fortnight on the whole trench line at any time after the Battle of the Somme the war might have ended— and what would mother have said then?

Colonel W.N. Nicholson

When my mother died, the world seemed just the same to me as it does now. The mystery of corpses pervading everything...

Max Beckmann, 1915

If you want to find the old battalion,
I know where they are, I know where they are,
I know where they are—
They're hanging on the old barbed wire,
I've seen 'em, I've seen 'em,
Hanging on the old barbed wire.

Voices From The Great War

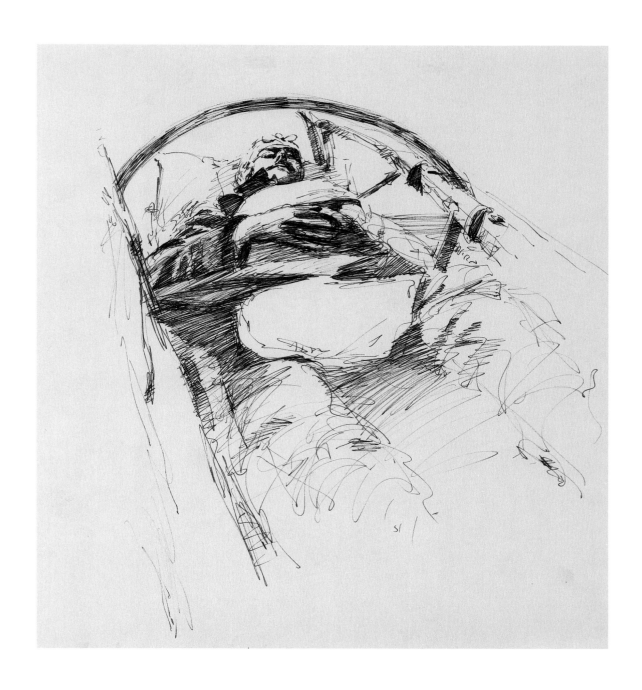

Here we dead lie because we did not choose
  To live and shame the land from which we sprung.
Life, to be sure, is nothing much to lose,
  But young men think it is, and we were young.

A.E. Housman

Everything has again been thrown into the tumultuous abyss to be melted down. The Past is relinquished, the Future shudders, the Present lacks foundations, but the hearts—should not they have the power to soar and hover among the mighty clouds?

Rainer Maria Rilke, 1914

I don't know what is to be done. This isn't war.
Lord Kitchener

The dead leaves float in the sighing air,
The darkness moves like a curtain drawn.
A veil which the morning sun will tear
From the face of death—we charge at dawn.

Patrick McGill

At least the thing will be over in three weeks.
Lieutenant Bernard Montgomery, 1914

I don't want to be a soldier,
I don't want to go to war.
I'd rather stay at home
Around the streets to roam
And live on the earnings of a fucking lady-typist.
I don't want a bayonet in my belly,
I don't want my bollocks shot away,
I'd rather stay in England,
In merry, merry England,
And fuck my bloody life away.

Voices From The Great War

But there may yet be a development in our understanding of the unspeakable wretchedness of our human life and perhaps all this is leading us to it; so much calamity—as though new dawns were seeking distance and space for their unfolding.

Rainer Maria Rilke, 1914

Honour has come back like a king to earth.
Rupert Brooke, 1914

To save your world you asked this
man to die:
Would this man, could he see you
now, ask why?

W.H. Auden, *Epitaph for an Unknown Soldier*

And two things have altered not
Since first the world began—
The beauty of the wild green earth
And the bravery of man.

T.P. Cameron Wilson

This war, like the next war, is a war to end war.

David Lloyd George, British Liberal statesman,
referring to the popular opinion that World War I
would be the last major war.

WATCH

A whole night,
thrown down beside a friend,
himself slaughtered,
his grinning mouth turned to the full moon,
I, with his convulsed hands reaching into my silence,
have written letters filled with love.
I have never felt so drawn towards life.

Giuseppe Ungaretti

"Good morning; Good morning!" the
general said
When we met him last week on our
way to the line.
Now the soldiers he smiled at are
most of 'em dead,
And we're cursing his staff for
incompetent swine.

Siegfried Sassoon, The General

Now all the roads lead to France
And heavy is the tread
Of the living; but the dead
Returning lightly dance.

Edward Thomas, Roads

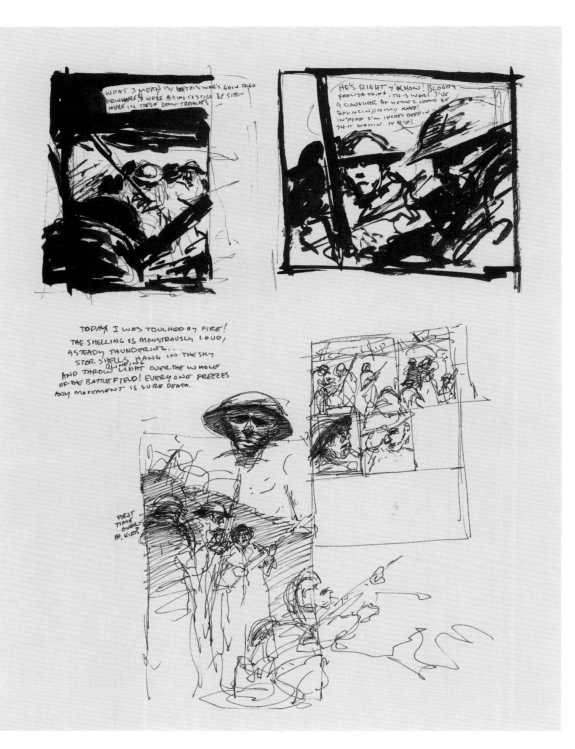

These are the quiet times. But sometimes the line wakes to fury. Guns flash and boom, the flares multiply in a madness of extravagance, and on the ear breaks the sound of a stupendous boiling. Sometimes the fury lasts for hours; sometimes it dies, as suddenly and inexplicably as it began, to the comparative quiet of the small arms again. But it leaves a hideous residue of maimed and slaughtered men, with their comrades appalled and shaken.

The Line alone, a moody giant, stretches his sinister length unmoved across the country.

2nd Lieutenant Ewart Richardson, 4th battalion, Princess of Wales' own (Yorkshire Regiment)

THE SCENE OF WAR; THE HAPPY WARRIOR

His wild heart beats with painful sobs,
His strained hands clench an ice-cold rifle,
His aching jaws grip a heart parched tongue,
And his wide eyes search unconsciously.

He cannot shriek.

Bloody saliva
Dribbles down his shapeless jacket.

I saw him stab
And stab again
A well-killed Boche.

This is the happy warrior,
This is he...

Herbert Read, 1916

I was frightened out of my life at nighttime. I was jellified, but I was more afraid of people knowing I was afraid—just a sort of bravado—I mustn't show them that I'm afraid—because one of the things that spreads quickest of all is fear. If people in trenches start to shout and scream with fear, it spreads like a flame, so the best thing is to quieten the bloke, either brain him or, if need be, finish him. Stop it.

Private C. Miles, 10th Battalion, Royal Fusiliers

Shells disinter the bodies, then reinter them, chop them to pieces, play with them as a cat plays with a mouse.

French observer, 1916

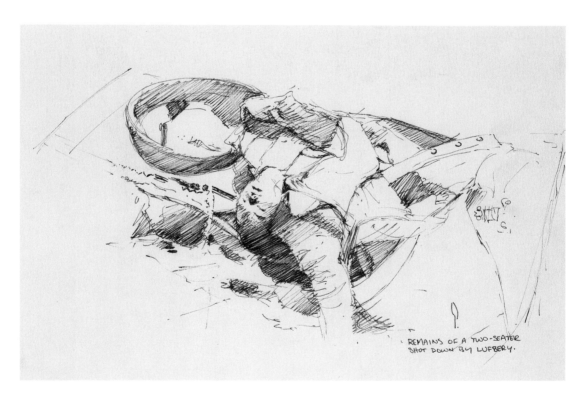

REMAINS OF A TWO-SEATER
SHOT DOWN BY LUFBERY.

Gas! Gas! Quick boys!—an ecstasy of fumbling.
Fitting the clumsy helmets just in time;
But someone still was yelling out and stumbling,
And flound'ring like a man in fire or lime...
Dim, through the misty panes and thick green light,
As under a green sea, I saw him drowning.

In all my dreams, before my helpless sight,
He plunges at me, guttering, choking, drowning.

Wilfred Owen

"Peace upon earth!" was said. We sing it,
  and pay a million priests to bring it.
After two thousand years of Mass
We've got as far as poison gas.

Thomas Hardy

And we are here as on a darkling plain
Swept with confused alarms of struggle and flight,
Where ignorant armies clash by night.

Matthew Arnold, Dover Beach

But that's what the young men are there for.
Adolph Hitler

If you could hear, at every jolt, the blood come gargling from the froth-corrupted lungs, obscene as cancer, bitter as the cud of vile incurable sores on innocent tongues, my friend, you would not tell with such high zest to children ardent for some desperate glory, the old Lie: *Dulce et decorum est pro patria mori.*

Wilfred Owen

But the men who left them thriftily to die in their own dung,
Shall they come with years and honour to the grave?

Rudyard Kipling

In 1916, one Frenchman in every 25 became a casualty.

The wind is level now, the earth is wet with dew,
The storm of stars in the sky will turn to quiet.
And soon all of us will sleep under the earth, we
Who never let each other sleep above it.
Maria Tsvetayeva, 1915

Mind you, they were a wonderful generation... let's face it, there were we, at the beginning of the war, the regular soldier, tough, hardened from India and South Africa, and then the 1st Army, Kitchener's... grand men they were. I watched a battalion of them march into battle on the Somme in 1916, and I thought to myself, "My God! What a wonderful lot of chaps." Fine physically, good, well set up, good marching... it was a good generation. It's a great pity it was decimated.

Sergeant W.J. Collins, Royal Army Medical Corps

DEAR SCOTT & PAM —
YOU TWO HAVE SEEN ME
THROUGH SOME TOUGH
TIMES. IF WE ARE

The Armistice was timed to commence at 11 a.m. on 11 November, and till that hour there was heavy firing from the German lines. A German machine-gun remained in action the whole morning opposite our lines. Just before 11 a.m., a thousand rounds were fired from it in a practically ceaseless burst. At five minutes to 11, the machine-gunner got up, took off his hat to us, and walked away.

At 11 a.m., there came great cheering from the German lines; and the village church bells rang. But on our side there were only a few shouts. I had heard more for a rum ration. The match was over; it had been a damned bad game.

Colonel W.N. Nicholson, Suffolk Regiment, Staff Officer attached, 15 Highland Division

THE HERO

"Jack fell as he'd have wished," the mother said,
And folded up the letter that she'd read.
"The Colonel writes so nicely." Something broke
In the tired voice that quivered to a choke.
She looked up. "We mothers are so proud
Of our dead soldiers." Then her face was bowed.

Quietly the Brother Officer went out.
He'd told the poor old dear some gallant lies
That she would nourish all her days, no doubt.
For while he coughed and mumbled, her weak eyes
Had shone with gentle triumph, brimmed with joy,
Because he'd been so brave, her glorious boy.

He thought how "Jack," cold-footed, useless swine,
Had panicked down the trench that night the mine
Went up at Wicked Corner; how he'd tried
To get sent home, and how, at last, he'd died,
Blown to small bits. And no one seemed to care
Except that lonely woman with white hair.

Siegfried Sassoon, 1917

GEORGE PRATT

Born October 13, 1960, in Beaumont, Texas, George Pratt moved to New York City in 1980 to study drawing and painting at Pratt Institute, where he now teaches.

His work has appeared in *Epic Illustrated, Heavy Metal, Eagle* magazine, and many other publications. He has done interior illustrations for Bantam Books, Ariel Books, and Kipling Press, and cover paintings for DC Comics.

A successful painter, he is represented by Grand Central Art Galleries, Inc. in New York City, and Jack Meier Gallery in Houston, Texas. His work is in private collections in the United States, England, France, Canada, Switzerland, and India, and has been exhibited in the Houston Museum of Fine Art.

He is currently working on *See You in Hell, Blind Boy; A Tale of the Blues* also for Tundra Publishing.